STEM Careers

Enhancing Engineering

Wendy Conklin, M.A.

Consultants

Timothy Rasinski, Ph.D.
Kent State University

Lori Oczkus, M.A.
Literacy Consultant

Publishing Credits

Rachelle Cracchiolo, M.S.Ed., *Publisher*
Conni Medina, M.A.Ed., *Managing Editor*
Dona Herweck Rice, *Series Developer*
Emily R. Smith, M.A.Ed., *Content Director*
Stephanie Bernard/Susan Daddis, M.A.Ed., *Editors*
Robin Erickson, *Senior Graphic Designer*

The TIME logo is a registered trademark of TIME Inc. Used under license.

Image Credits: pp. 12–13 S-F/Shutterstock.com; pp. 14–15 bukharova/
iStock.com; p. 25 NASA; p. 31 Cultura Creative (RF)/Alamy Stock Photo; pp.
32–33 Hero Images/Getty Images; pp. 36–37 Tetra Images/Getty Images;
p. 37 Mary Evans Picture Library/Alamy Stock Photo; pp. 38–39 Used with
permission of Inter IKEA Systems B.V.; pp. 42–43 Chad Baker/Getty Images;
all other images from iStock and/or Shutterstock.

Library of Congress Cataloging-in-Publication Data

Names: Conklin, Wendy, author.
Title: STEM careers. Enhancing engineering / Wendy Conklin, M.A.
Other titles: Enhancing engineering
Description: Huntington Beach, CA : Teacher Created Materials, Inc., [2017] |
  Audience: Grades 7 to 8. | Includes bibliographical references and index.
Identifiers: LCCN 2016031448 (print) | LCCN 2016034559 (ebook) | ISBN
  9781493836222 (pbk.) | ISBN 9781480757264 (eBook)
Subjects: LCSH: Engineering--Juvenile literature. | Engineering--Vocational
  guidance--Juvenile literature.
Classification: LCC TA157 .C5735 2017 (print) | LCC TA157 (ebook) | DDC
  620--dc23
LC record available at https://lccn.loc.gov/2016031448

Teacher Created Materials

5301 Oceanus Drive
Huntington Beach, CA 92649-1030
http://www.tcmpub.com

ISBN 978-1-4938-3622-2

© 2017 Teacher Created Materials, Inc.
Printed in China
YiCai.032019.CA201901471

Table of Contents

Engineering Builds a Better World 4

Doing the Job of an Engineer. 6

The Engineering Design Process 20

Technology and Engineering
Go Hand in Hand 36

Engineering the Future. 42

Glossary 44

Index 45

Check It Out! 46

Try It! 47

About the Author. 48

Engineering Builds a Better World

Imagine you owned a robot that could sense a human's mood and emotions. What if someday you lived on the moon—or better yet, Mars? Or, if your favorite pet dies, you have it cloned so that you can have another pet *exactly* like it. If any of this intrigues you, you might want to consider becoming an engineer.

Engineering is the field of technology where people come up with new ideas, build them, and then test their ideas. While an engineer is not strictly a scientist, engineering has a lot to do with science. A scientist observes things and has **theoretical** ideas. Engineers build machines, structures such as bridges or roads, and systems found in video games and smart phones. Engineering is applying science to solve problems in our everyday lives. It's *doing* science, but engineering also involves math, design, psychology, and creativity.

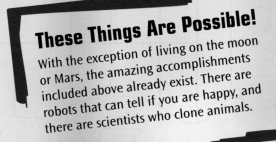

These Things Are Possible!

With the exception of living on the moon or Mars, the amazing accomplishments included above already exist. There are robots that can tell if you are happy, and there are scientists who clone animals.

THINK LINK

- What are some things you use every day that an engineer designed?
- How have advancing technologies created new jobs or transformed old ones in engineering?
- How would our lives be different if there were no engineers?

Doing the Job of an Engineer

Engineers design and build things such as driveways, computer software, and flying suits. But, to say that someone is an engineer doesn't give us a clear idea of what he or she does beyond designing and building. The designing and building process involves steps and takes time.

Engineers affect our everyday lives. For example, think about the features on a smart phone and how these features improve our lives. Engineers came up with these ideas. They built **prototypes** based on their ideas, and then they tested these ideas to see if they worked. Many times, engineers have to "go back to the drawing board" by changing their ideas or completely starting over. It becomes a trial-and-error process.

There are more than 200 different **disciplines** or fields of engineering. These fields are divided into four main branches. The branches are chemical, civil, electrical, and mechanical.

The Roads Around You

Do you ever see roads under construction? Transportation engineers are involved in this construction. They are the people who plan, design, and upgrade streets and highways.

Fore!

The game of golf, as we know it today, began in Scotland in the 1450s. Since then, the golf ball has gone through its own evolution. First, it was made with feathers, then rubber. Throughout these changes, the different designs were tested. Balls made with indentations went farther than those without. In 1905, William Taylor, an English engineer, **patented** the dimples that are on golf balls.

Disciplines of Engineering

Engineering offers a wide variety of exciting career choices. Here are some specialized disciplines organized under the four main engineering branches:

Chemical Engineering

- ceramic engineering
- materials engineering
- paper engineering
- plastics engineering
- petroleum engineering

Civil Engineering

- architectural engineering
- construction engineering
- earthquake engineering
- ecological engineering
- environmental engineering
- fire protection engineering
- geotechnical engineering
- highway engineering
- hydraulic engineering
- mining engineering
- railway engineering
- structural engineering
- traffic engineering
- transportation engineering
- water resource engineering

Electrical Engineering

- computer engineering
- control engineering
- electronics engineering
- microelectronics engineering
- power engineering
- software engineering
- telecommunications engineering

Mechanical Engineering

- acoustic engineering
- aerospace engineering
- audio engineering
- automotive engineering
- manufacturing engineering
- marine engineering
- nuclear engineering
- thermal engineering

Chemical Engineering

Think about your favorite toys when you were young. With the exception of stuffed animals, the toys were most likely made from plastic. You can thank a chemical engineer for those toys!

Chemical engineers create better plastics, paper, paint, medicine, and fuel. Their jobs include, for example, designing plastic toys that are both safe and fun for children. Have you ever been in a freshly painted room and smelled strong chemicals? Chemical engineers work to create **nontoxic** paint so that people don't get sick from the fumes. They take lumber and bark and turn them into paper products such as notepads and cardboard. These engineers also work to build more fuel-efficient vehicles.

Snurfin' U.S.A.

In 1965, Sherman Poppen's daughters were fidgety. Being an engineer, he put two skis together and sent his girls outside to try them. After watching them stand on his contraption going downhill, he replaced the skis with one board and attached a rope to the front for steering. His wife combined the words *snow* and *surf* to name the contraption a Snurfer. Many people believe Poppen's invention contributed to the design of snowboards.

Petroleum engineering is a type of chemical engineering. These engineers produce fuels for vehicles and machinery. They focus on the processes and equipment used to refine oil into a form that is usable. Petroleum engineers figure out strategies for extracting oil from wells. And they focus on how to drill to get the oil safely.

You will find chemical engineers working with mining, oil companies, **pharmaceutical**, and food production companies.

Geology Rocks!

Petroleum engineers have to know geology to do their jobs safely. They need to know what types of rocks they are drilling into. They also have to know about the **properties** of metal in the bits they use during drilling.

Civil Engineering

If you like organizing and planning big projects, civil engineering might be great for you. Civil engineers have designed a tunnel that could cross the Bering Strait. The tunnel would span about 60 miles (96.5 kilometers) and connect Russia and Alaska. Other engineers have drafted a plan for Tokyo's Sky City 1000. This high-rise city with apartments, offices, theaters, and schools will house approximately 35,000 people.

Imagine a city within a pyramid! Civil engineers have proposed that, too. It is called the Mega-City Pyramid, and the plans are to build it over Tokyo Bay in Japan. About one million people will be able to live there.

While these projects are in the designing and testing phases, the Burj Al Arab is a reality. It is a luxury hotel in Dubai. It stands 1,050 feet (320 meters) tall, and the hotel's restaurant is suspended 82 feet (25 meters) away from the main building.

Civil engineers figure out how to build these amazing structures and make them safe. They have to understand how weather affects the materials they use. If it rains, will the saturation of water affect the building? If the ground swells, will the structure be compromised? They also must know the chemical properties of the metals they use. **Ferrous metals** like steel are strong but heavy. **Nonferrous metals** are also strong but much lighter.

Lessons Learned from 9/11

After the Twin Towers of the World Trade Center collapsed on September 11, 2001, civil engineers explored more ways to protect people. While no building may be able to withstand a plane's impact, engineers can design shelters within high rises where people can wait out fires or other disasters. They also are designing buildings that won't collapse due to fires.

Burj Al Arab Hotel in Dubai

THINK LINK

◎ Why would a civil engineer need a strong background in math and science when designing a tall building?

◎ If a civil engineer makes a mistake on the types of materials used in a building, what might happen?

◎ How can civil engineers learn from structures built long ago?

Clean Rooms

When working on microchips, electrical engineers have to think about contamination. They must work in clean rooms that are free of dust and other particles. **Impurities** on microchips will ruin them.

Electrical Engineering

Have you ever ridden a roller coaster and felt a funny feeling in your stomach? Electrical engineers have a lot to do with making a ride thrilling but also safe for riders. It takes electricity to help create the thrills and chills.

Electricity is used everywhere. We use it to communicate with others. Movie theaters use it to show the latest films. Hospitals use it to power the machines that keep people alive and well.

Electrical engineers must understand all about electricity and how it works. To do this, they should have a good understanding of atoms. Atoms contain electrons that when moved from one atom to another, create electricity. Engineers choose materials based on how much current is needed. Materials that conduct electricity allow it to flow freely. Electrical engineers understand how to harness the power of an electrical charge. They make the electricity flow safely so that it can power up gadgets of all kinds.

Electrical engineers design computer circuits. They also develop and test electrical equipment in navigation and communication systems. They devise power grids and work on power supplies. And right now, they are designing the next big thing in electronics! Who knows what it will be?

Working on a Small Scale

A microelectronics engineer works on microchips that are programmed to make computers, phones, and other devices perform tasks. Many pets have microchips in their skin to identify them if they get lost. These microchips are about the size of a grain of rice.

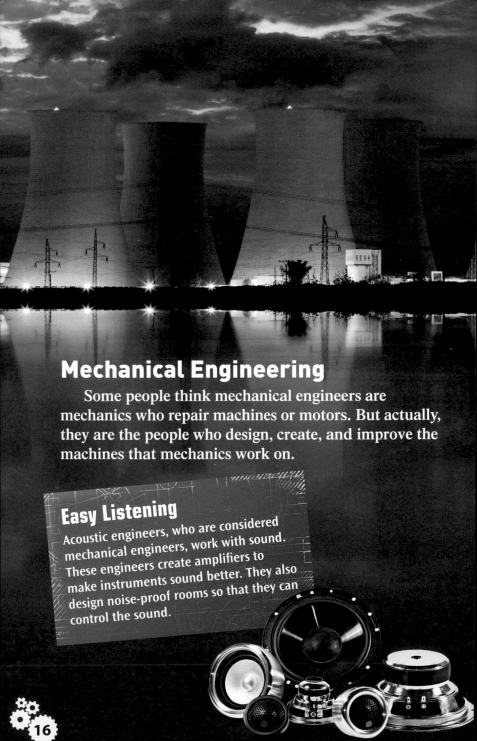

Mechanical Engineering

Some people think mechanical engineers are mechanics who repair machines or motors. But actually, they are the people who design, create, and improve the machines that mechanics work on.

Easy Listening

Acoustic engineers, who are considered mechanical engineers, work with sound. These engineers create amplifiers to make instruments sound better. They also design noise-proof rooms so that they can control the sound.

Nuclear Power

Nuclear engineering is a part of mechanical engineering. These engineers design nuclear power plants and reactors. They also develop weapons and conduct radiation research. Although nuclear power has some advantages, there are environmental and health concerns related to its use.

In general, mechanical engineering has to do with things that move. Mechanical engineers designed the flight hardware of NASA's *Orion* spacecraft. NASA is hopeful it will take astronauts to Mars someday. Think of your favorite music. A type of mechanical engineer mixed the sounds to get the music you enjoy. What car features might not have existed when your parents were young? Mechanical engineers designed these improvements.

Mechanical engineers have to understand the physical properties of materials. How much stress and strain can a material handle? Is the material hard enough? Will it function well? These are just some of the questions that mechanical engineers think about when designing.

Other Fields of Engineering

Some engineering fields do not fall under the four main branches. Wind and biomedical engineering are two such examples. Others include tissue and food engineering.

Have you ever seen large white **turbines** in an open field? Wind engineers build these turbines. The turbines produce energy. Together, structural and energy-related engineers work to make this happen.

Biomedical engineers work with scientists and medical personnel. They design machines, software, and artificial body parts that help patients. Many people lose limbs due to accidents or infections. These engineers design **prosthetic** limbs. They also design MRI technology and powerful x-ray machines. Doctors use these machines to diagnose patients' problems.

Tissue engineers can create organs. They combine cells to replace, reuse, or restore body tissue. Doctors rely on them to design artificial organs for transplants into humans.

Food engineers work to keep food production safe and healthy. They also genetically modify foods. For example, they create seeds that can survive in areas that suffer from severe drought. There are obvious benefits to this. There is also debate about whether such changes are truly healthy.

Burning Rubber

Running is an activity that many people enjoy. However, with all of the pounding on roads, trails, or treadmills, running can be hard on joints and muscles. Enter biomechanical engineers. These men and women study humans in motion. When they design shoes, besides fit, they must consider some other important features, such as flexibility, thickness of sole, grip, and weight.

The Engineering Design Process

Have you ever considered the idea that to succeed you need to fail a few times? Many people are afraid of failure—for a good reason. Failure doesn't feel good; on the other hand, success *does* feel good. But engineers depend on failure to guide them toward success. Without failure, they cannot succeed. Failure is a necessary step in solving problems.

The design process is a series of steps that engineers use as they design and build things. While there are many different design processes that an engineer can use, they all have steps in common and generally lead to the same outcome.

The Scientific Method

The engineering design process is different from the scientific method, but these processes do have similarities.

The Engineering Design Process	The Scientific Method
Identify the problem.	
Brainstorm ideas.	State the question.
Design a prototype.	Formulate a hypothesis.
Build models.	Design an experiment.
Test and evaluate.	Experiment.
Present the solution.	Analyze the results.
	Communicate the results.

STOP! THINK...

- According to the chart, what are the differences between the engineering design process and the scientific method?

- Why are these differences important?

- What would happen if an engineer used the scientific method instead of the design process when solving a problem?

21

The Design Process

Identify the Problem

Ask if the problem is valid. Is it justified? Is it a real problem? Get a clear focus on what the problem is to be able to generate solutions. Write a problem statement.

Present the Solution

What will the presentation look like? It could be in the form of a report or a display board, hard copy or digital. The presentation should include the research, data collected, and ultimate solution.

Redesign

What tweaks must be made to improve it? Make any necessary changes to your design. You may want to retest and evaluate to ensure success with the updated design.

Test and Evaluate

Does the solution solve the problem? Send your final design to your users. Gather their feedback to decide what needs to be adjusted, fixed, or deleted.

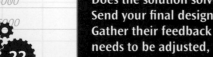

Brainstorm Ideas

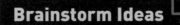

Research and brainstorm ideas to solve the problem. Find out if technology already exists to support the ideas. Sometimes, this means redefining the problem.

Design a Prototype

Evaluate the ideas to weed out the options that don't work from the ones that might. Determine the best solution, and design a prototype.

Build Models

Build a prototype. Use your creativity and imagination. The materials used in this step are less expensive and easier to handle than materials in the final version.

Identify the Problem

Engineers design and build things to solve problems. The design process for engineers always starts with a problem. They have to understand a problem completely before a solution can be given. Engineers have to know what they are trying to solve.

For example, engineers at NASA wanted to create an outpost for astronauts on the moon. The astronauts needed to land near the outpost. Lunar landers carried supplies to the astronauts there. But the engine kicked up dust and dirt, which harmed the cargo, when the lunar lander hit the moon's surface. So, the engineers decided to place the cargo on top of the lander to protect it. The problem was that they needed a device that could reach the cargo on the top of the lander and transport that cargo to the outpost.

Understanding this problem and working through the design challenges led them to create the ATHLETE vehicle. ATHLETE stands for All-Terrain, Hex Limbed, Extra-Terrestrial Explorer. These engineers would not have been able to create the ATHLETE to solve the problem if they had not first understood the problem. Once the problem has been identified, a problem statement or definition can be written.

Paving the Way

Mae C. Jemison graduated from Stanford University in 1977 with a chemical engineering degree and from Cornell University in 1981 with a medical degree. When she applied for NASA's astronaut training program in 1987, she, along with 14 other candidates, was chosen out of 2,000 applicants. On September 12, 1992, Jemison became the first African American woman to go on a mission to space. She studied the effects of weightlessness and nausea in space using the other six crew members and herself.

NASA's ATHLETE

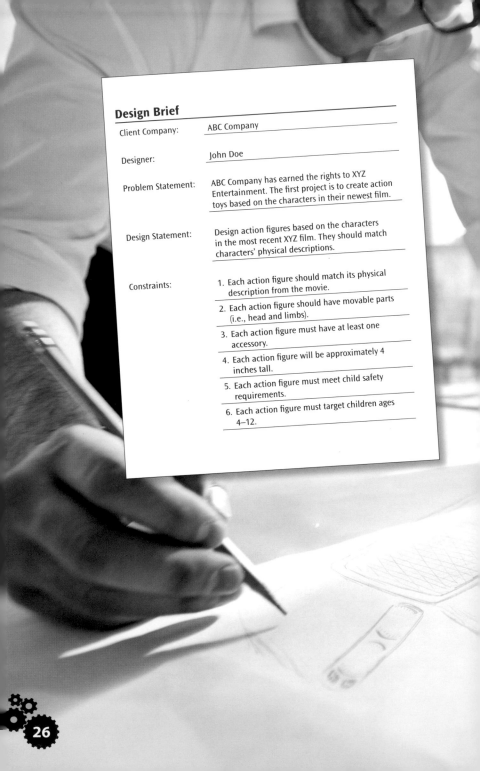

Design Brief

Client Company: ABC Company

Designer: John Doe

Problem Statement: ABC Company has earned the rights to XYZ Entertainment. The first project is to create action toys based on the characters in their newest film.

Design Statement: Design action figures based on the characters in the most recent XYZ film. They should match characters' physical descriptions.

Constraints:
1. Each action figure should match its physical description from the movie.
2. Each action figure should have movable parts (i.e., head and limbs).
3. Each action figure must have at least one accessory.
4. Each action figure will be approximately 4 inches tall.
5. Each action figure must meet child safety requirements.
6. Each action figure must target children ages 4–12.

Gather Information

Next, engineers complete a **design brief**. This is a document that contains all the important information for solving the problem. The brief identifies the client, the end user, the problem statement, the design statement, the criteria or constraints, and a list of the **deliverables**.

- The client is the person or government hiring the engineer to solve the problem.

- The end user is the person or people who will use the product.

- The problem statement identifies what the problem is, but it does not include the solution.

- The design statement says what the engineer will do to solve the problem.

- The criteria or constraints tell when the project is due, how much money can be spent, materials that can be used, and what it needs to look like.

- The list of deliverables tells what the engineer will give to the client. Will it be a prototype or just a series of drawings? Will the client receive a presentation board or something else?

Meeting Needs

Engineers need to think of all possible needs of the end users. It is important for engineers to consider questions such as: "Who is this for?" "What is the purpose of this project/product?" and "What is the budget?"

Brainstorm Ideas

Once there is a clear understanding of the problem, engineers brainstorm to solve it. Brainstorming is the act of listing ideas. All ideas are encouraged. At times, one idea may lead to another or to a combination of ideas. Engineers do not judge ideas at this stage.

Engineers may brainstorm in groups or individually. Many brains are often better than one; so brainstorming with others can yield more ideas.

Often, engineers conduct additional research at this point. They may investigate to find out if technology already exists for their ideas to work. Other times, the brainstorming does not produce any solutions. Then, engineers return to defining the problem. They may find they were looking at the wrong things the first time around. They may interview or observe people who are affected by the problem, which gives them a better understanding of the problem and how it can be fixed.

Engineers also take closer looks at solutions that already exist and ask why these solutions are not working. Then, they refine their ideas. The teams narrow the ideas and vote on them or use a **decision matrix** to select the best solution.

Wheels in Motion

The World's Fair was coming to Chicago in 1893, and George W. Ferris, an engineer from Pittsburgh, was intrigued. He designed a ride attraction, sometimes known as "giant wheels." At first, it was rejected because of safety issues. He eventually found architects to help him build it. The rotating wheel was 250 feet (76.2 meters) in diameter and had 36 cars. The cost for a 20-minute ride was 50 cents!

Design Prototypes

Engineers need to show their clients what the solution looks like and give the clients something tangible to see and consider. To do this, they may use isometric drawings. Isometrics are 2-D drawings that show perspective. They are like visual prototypes. Engineers may use one- or two-point perspective drawings. Multi-view drawings show two or more dimensions of a 3-D object. After drawing initial sketches, the engineer creates technical drawings that use exact measurements. Then, the client can really visualize and understand the design.

Engineers Improve a Shopping Cart

An engineering firm was given the task to make shopping carts less desirable to steal. One solution was to create removable buckets with handles that fit into an open frame of a cart. When the buckets were removed at checkout, the cart could not carry anything except grocery bags that hung on hooks. So, the carts were not desirable for thieves.

Next, engineers use computer programs with 3-D software to make models. From these models, engineers study the shapes and texture. They try to identify flaws. The sketches and computer models help engineers select materials. Engineers have to make sure that the technology exists or can be created to build the prototypes. And then they decide what types of manufacturing methods can be used for the product.

Build, Test, and Evaluate

Engineers build prototypes from the working drawings and computer models. Understanding physical properties of materials is important as they decide on the best materials to use. The materials need to hold up against stress, force, and strains. Once built, all prototypes are tested to see how well they perform the necessary functions. Engineers think about the types of tests they must run to get reliable data. As they gather data from these experiments, they report findings to their teams. The teams critique the designs to find shortcomings and concerns. Then, they redesign.

Engineers may need to rebuild the prototype completely or simply modify it from its original state. Then, they test it again and gather more data. Once the design is right, engineers look for consistent performance results and update their data. They also have users try it out to see how it works and how the users respond. These users provide valuable feedback on the design. All this information tells engineers whether they have met the criteria on the design brief. Once the results are consistent and the user feedback is positive, engineers know they have a solution to the problem.

Safer Places

Industrial engineers strive to make workplace environments safer and more productive. When designing solutions for clients, they rely heavily on computer-generated models. Computer **simulations** help them understand how to improve the functions of a location.

Present the Solution

Finally, engineers present the solution to the clients. These solutions come in the form of deliverables. In essence, deliverables are what the engineer delivers to the client. Depending on the expectations set forth in the design brief, engineers might use media such as design boards, computer-presentation software, and technical reports to show the solutions. These display their drawings and the data they collected. Engineers also present the final models and prototypes.

Many solutions are technology driven. For example, one engineering firm worked on the problem of improving the health of people in a community. They did their research and discovered that many people in this particular community could not afford expensive health and fitness equipment or exercise club memberships. So, they presented the client with smartphone apps as prototypes. These apps were more affordable, each costing only a few dollars. One of these apps had the user put in the food he or she was craving at that moment. Then, the app told the user alternative foods to eat that were healthier. Another app allowed the user to place grocery store orders. Then, the app gave sample menus for healthy meals based on the order.

Appetizing Apps

There are many health and fitness apps available for smartphones. One app helps users track their nutrition goals by scanning foods. Once scanned, the app determines whether foods are in the best interest of the user's goals. It can scan a variety of produce and packaged foods. A reward system is included to encourage healthier minds and bodies.

That's Hairy

One vending machine prototype analyzes a person's nutritional needs by testing a hair sample. Then, the machine creates the perfect healthy smoothie for that person. Engineers also hope to create a vending machine that can test a diabetic person's blood and then offer a snack based on the sample.

Technology and Engineering Go Hand in Hand

Back in 230 BC, a Greek mathematician named Archimedes designed an elevator with ropes and pulleys that could lift one person. In the second century AD, a machine with a crane and a large wheel helped build a tomb in ancient Rome. Enslaved people turned the wheel at the base and lifted the materials into the air. Years later, Leonardo da Vinci sketched ideas to help people fly. These drawings include images of what we know today as helicopters. The technology did not exist at that time to make human flight a reality. But as time moved forward, technology advanced. This advancement enabled engineers to design and build vehicles that fly.

Does technology advance engineering, or is it the other way around? The wheel was one of the first technologies known to man. It allowed people to move large stones and build the amazing pyramids of Egypt. But first, an early engineer had to create the tools that could make a wheel. In this case, engineering advanced technology.

Improving Flight Over Time

In 1903, Wilbur and Orville Wright became the first people to fly a motor-powered plane successfully. By World War I, ace pilots flew planes over enemy territory, but these planes were not very reliable. Planes are more reliable today because engineers continually improve them.

Interesting Prototypes in the Works

Some engineers work on solutions for the future. They know that the technology does not exist yet, but that doesn't stop them from inventing new ideas for products.

Take for example the popular store IKEA. The company wants to design a table for the future that can serve many functions. Using a camera mounted above the table, the table would be able to recognize the types of foods placed on its surface. The camera would then project onto the table various recipes and cooking tips for using that food. To ensure accurate measurements, the table could weigh each ingredient. It would know how to cook the food appropriately, such as boiling or frying, and could even keep a coffee cup warm. Cooks would be able to browse recipes and record their own cooking sessions at this table.

To create this table, engineers have to determine brand-new technologies that don't exist today. This new table will affect the way people live in the future. It will affect future kitchen designs, and it will impact the types of foods we cook. The engineers are not only designing something new and interesting, they are changing how we live.

Time to Cook

How would this new cooking table work? Users choose a recipe. Then, they set a timer based on how much time they want to spend cooking. The table makes suggestions about which recipes to follow.

More Functions

This table of the future is being designed to charge mobile devices. It will even encourage physical activities for young children.

Planned to Fail

Did you know that engineers control the release of technology to the public? Believe it or not, some products are designed and built to fail. This is called planned obsolescence. Think of a computer and how it wears out after a few years. It may go slower or suddenly shut down for no apparent reason. Over time, the technology changes, and new software is needed to keep the computer up to date. Engineers design products such as computers, cars, and video games to expire or become obsolete within a few years. For example, video game systems are released without their full computing potential. That is because manufacturers want to unleash the power over time. They engineer each phase of the technology with a projected end in sight. In the meantime, they work on building the next system, which will have stronger capabilities.

Why do they do this? In some cases, the materials required to build a lasting product would be too expensive for anyone to afford. In other cases, companies want to make more money, so they need ways to create more products that consumers have to buy. In the case of video gaming systems, often old games won't work on the new systems, so consumers have to buy new versions of the games to keep playing them.

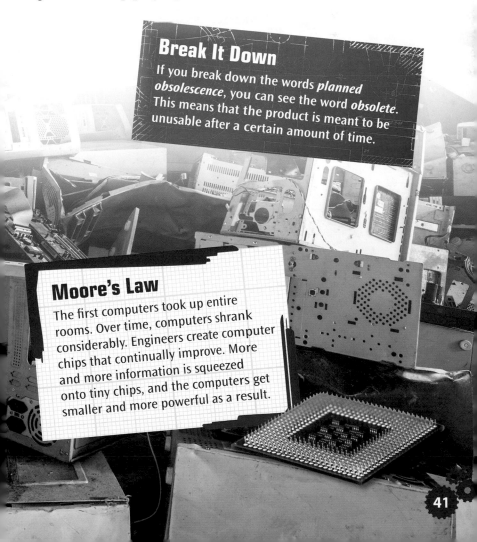

Break It Down

If you break down the words *planned obsolescence*, you can see the word *obsolete*. This means that the product is meant to be unusable after a certain amount of time.

Moore's Law

The first computers took up entire rooms. Over time, computers shrank considerably. Engineers create computer chips that continually improve. More and more information is squeezed onto tiny chips, and the computers get smaller and more powerful as a result.

Engineering the Future

Engineers are looking to provide energy solutions that protect the environment for the future. For example, they will continue to design more fuel-efficient vehicles. Engineers work with scientists to design hydrogen-powered fuel cells. These fuel cells are carbon-free systems that power electric motors. Engineers hope these fuel cells will power the vehicles of the future. Right now, the technology is too expensive. But some people predict that if we plan well, most people will be driving these vehicles by 2040.

New Branches of Engineering

The problems we encounter will predict what types of engineering is needed in the future. Many people believe that environmental engineering will soon become its own branch with many fields under it.

So, does technology advance engineers? Or do engineers advance technology? Perhaps engineering and technology help to advance each other. It is difficult to separate the two. It takes engineering to develop technology. Technology has to be there for engineers to use. So, the next time you pick up a phone, ride in a car, or turn on the lights, stop to reflect. Think about the technology, and consider all the work engineers do to make these things possible.

Glossary

decision matrix—a chart that helps team members identify priorities when working on projects

deliverables—materials like design boards, drawings, video concepts, and prototypes that engineers give to clients after solving problems

design brief—the document that has all the information designers use when solving problems for clients

disciplines—fields or areas of engineering

ferrous metals—metals that are mostly made of iron

impurities—substances that contaminate

nonferrous metals—metals that don't contain iron

nontoxic—nonpoisonous, safe materials

patented—earned the sole rights to an invention

petroleum—crude oil found in the earth

pharmaceutical—prescription drug

properties—qualities, traits, or attributes

prosthetic—a man-made device that replaces a missing human body part, such as a limb

prototypes—models of designed products

simulations—enactments of something meant to be tests

theoretical—hypothetical ideas, existing in theory only

turbines—engines powered by steam or gas that make large blades turn

Index

acoustic engineer, 9,16

Archimedes, 36

ATHLETE, 24–25

Bering Strait, 12

Burj Al Arab Hotel, 12–13

chemical engineering, 6, 8, 10–11, 25

civil engineering, 6, 8, 12–13

da Vinci, Leonardo, 36

design brief, 26–27, 33–34

design process, 20–24

Dubai, 12–13

electrical engineering, 6, 9, 14–15

environmental engineering, 8, 42

Ferris, George W., 28

fields of engineering, 6, 18–19

IKEA, 38

industrial engineers, 33

Jemison, Mae C., 25

mechanical engineering, 6, 9, 16–17

Mega-City Pyramid, 12

microchips, 14–15

microelectronics, 9, 15

Moore's Law, 41

NASA, 17, 24–25

nuclear engineering, 9, 17

Orion spacecraft, 17

petroleum engineering, 8, 11

Poppen, Sherman, 10

prototype, 6, 21, 23, 27, 30–31, 33–35, 38

scientific method, 21

Snurfer, 10

Tokyo's Sky City, 12

transportation engineers, 7

Twin Towers, 13

World War I, 37

Wright, Wilbur and Orville, 37

Check It Out!

Books

Biskup, Agnieszka. 2013. *The Incredible World of Engineers with Max Axiom, Super Scientist.* Capstone Press.

Brasch, Nicolas. 2013. *Triumphs of Engineering.* PowerKids Press.

Farmer, Nancy. 2002. *The House of the Scorpion.* Russel Gordon Atheneum Books.

Herweck, Don. 2007. *All About Mechanical Engineering.* Teacher Created Materials.

Kroll, Jennifer. 2013. *The Cutting Edge: Breakthroughs in Technology.* Teacher Created Materials.

LeBoutillier, Linda. 2015. *Unusual and Awesome Jobs Using Technology.* Capstone Press.

Woolston, Blythe. 2012. *Catch & Release.* Carolrhoda Lab.

Videos

Lorenz, Jennifer. *Extreme Engineering Series.* Discovery Channel.

Modern Marvels Season 5. A&E Television Networks.

Websites

Engineering.com. http://www.engineering.com/.

National Academy of Engineering. *Greatest Engineering Achievements of the 20th Century.* http://www.greatachievements.org/.

Try It!

Imagine you are an engineer hired to design a new toy, bridge, roller coaster, or something in your local community.

- ⊚ First, decide what type of engineer you would like to be.

- ⊚ Next, choose what you would like to design for your community.

- ⊚ Follow the steps through the engineering design process on pages 22–23 to guide you.

- ⊚ After all your hard work, share your design presentation with an audience.

About the Author

Besides writing books for students and conducting training sessions for teachers, Wendy Conklin has a wide variety of interests, from reviving old furniture to competing in rigorous athletic competitions. If there's a challenge, she jumps in to take it on. Her motto is to live life to the fullest and have no regrets. Someday, she hopes to live in Hawaii, but right now, she lives with her family and two sweet Boston terriers in Round Rock, Texas.